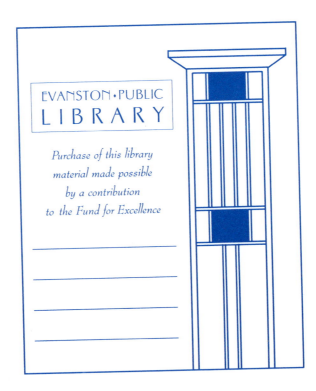

EVANSTON·PUBLIC
LIBRARY

*Purchase of this library
material made possible
by a contribution
to the Fund for Excellence*

Mythology

Mythology

ANNE WRIGHT

Sharpe Focus
an imprint of M.E. Sharpe, Inc.

First edition for the United States, its territories and dependencies,
Canada, Mexico, and Australia, published in 2008 by M.E. Sharpe, Inc.

Sharpe Focus
An imprint of M.E. Sharpe, Inc.
80 Business Park Drive
Armonk, NY 10504

www.mesharpe.com

Library of Congress Cataloging-in-Publication Data

Wright, Anne Margaret.
   Mythology / Anne Wright.
      p. cm. -- (Inside ancient Greece)
   Includes bibliographical references and index.
   ISBN 978-0-7656-8132-4 (hardcover : alk. paper)
   1. Mythology, Greek. I. Title.

BL783.W75 2008
292.1'3--dc22
                         2007011419

Editorial and design by Amber Books Ltd
Project Editor: James Bennett
Copy Editor: Deborah Murrell
Picture Research: Kate Green
Design: Andrew Easton

Cover Design: Jesse Sanchez, M.E. Sharpe, Inc.

Printed in Malaysia

9 8 7 6 5 4 3 2 1

For T, Βασιλευς Βασιλεων
and for F, my little angel.

PICTURE CREDITS

AKG-Images: 6–7, 14–15, 20, 24, 26, 28(b), 29, 31, 33, 34, 38, 42–43, 44, 45, 57, 60, 62, 64, 65, 66, 72, 73, 75
Corbis: 22, 28(t), 46, 48, 58, 61, 71
De Agostini: 8, 10, 11(both), 13, 16–17, 19, 23, 27, 30, 36, 37, 41, 49, 50, 52, 54, 55, 56, 63, 68, 70

ABOUT THE AUTHOR

Anne Wright gained a First Class Honours degree from the University of St. Andrews, Scotland,
before moving on to further study at Corpus Christi College, University of Oxford. After teaching in
London, she moved back to Oxford, where she is currently Head of Classics at Summer Fields, an
independent boys' boarding school. She lives in Oxford, U.K.

Contents

Introduction

The civilization of the ancient Greeks has influenced the world for thousands of years. Much of what we take for granted today, in areas such as science, mathematics, drama, poetry, and philosophy, was invented by the ancient Greeks. In many other fields, too, the Greeks made huge advances in human knowledge. Modern politicians still look for inspiration to fifth-century B.C.E. Athens, the cradle of democracy. Ancient Greek plays are still performed today, and in all the major cities of the world you can find buildings heavily influenced by Greek architecture. This series of books explores the full richness of Greek culture and history. It also considers how Greek civilization still influences us today.

Ancient Greek Religion

Much of Greek religion may appear strange to us today. There were many different gods and they were often cruel and unkind. However, these gods were very important to the Greeks and splendid temples and sanctuaries were built in their honor. The Greeks also held great festivals to pay tribute to their gods. As well as being a time of feasting and celebration, many of these festivals were also the venue for competitions in music, poetry, drama, and athletics. This book introduces the main Greek gods, how the gods were believed to influence everyday life, and how the Greeks worshipped them.

Many of the myths and legends of the ancient Greeks are set in Greece. However, some reflect the fact that the Greeks traveled widely and liked to hear exciting tales about the perils of travel and exploration. For example, Odysseus was to face terrible dangers at the Straits of Messina, in Italy, and Heracles traveled widely during his labors, including to the distant Atlas mountains in north Africa.

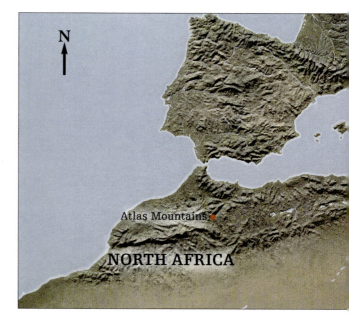

Mythology

The ancient Greeks liked to tell myths to explain how the world worked. Sometimes these stories were used to account for events, such as earthquakes or the seasons of the year. At other times, the myths explored human emotions and tried to explain why humans might be unkind or unhappy. Greek legends also told of the exciting adventures of their heroes, people who were supposed to have lived in the distant past such as Odysseus, who traveled for ten years, battling against monsters, or Theseus, who killed the terrible Minotaur, which was half-man and half-bull. This book tells these strange tales and wonderful adventures.

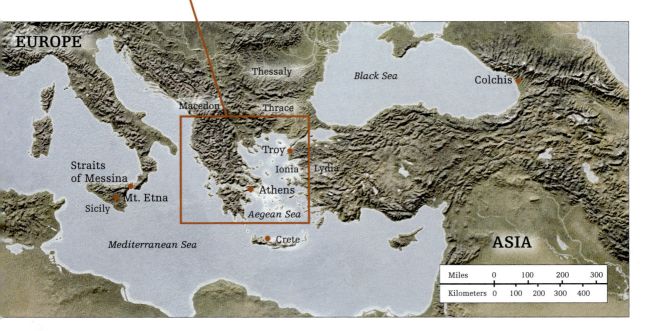

Chapter One

Religion

What Was Greek "Religion?"

The ancient Greeks were a very god-fearing people. Their gods were generally uninterested in human happiness and could be extremely unpleasant to people and to each other. Therefore the Greeks believed that it was very important to keep the gods happy with sacrifices and ceremonies. The ancient Greeks did not have a religion as we often think of religions today. They had no sacred book, no official church, and not even a specific word meaning "religion." People in different parts of Greece prayed to different gods, and the same god might have many different roles to which people could appeal.

The Olympian Gods

The most important gods were called the Olympian gods, and were said to live on Mount Olympus (*Oh-LIM-puss*) in northern Greece. The ruler of the gods was **Zeus** (*Zooss*), and he was married to **Hera** (*HAY-ra*), who was the goddess of childbirth, women, and marriage. Zeus is often seen in pictures armed with a thunderbolt, and he was believed to hurl thunderbolts down to earth when he was angry. Although Zeus was not a very considerate god (he often neglected his wife and made her very unhappy), the Greeks believed that this reflected the problems of human nature. His most important roles were as the defender of law and justice, and protector of families.

The Parthenon in Athens is one of the most famous buildings in Greece. This temple was built in the fifth century B.C.E. and was dedicated to Athena, the patron goddess of Athens.

Aphrodite (*Aff-ro-DIE-tee*) was the goddess of love and was married to **Hephaestus** (*Heff-EYE-stuss*), who was the god of fire and the blacksmith to the gods. Hephaestus was the son of Zeus and Hera, and was lame. The Greeks said that Hephaestus was injured when he was thrown down from heaven in one of Zeus' rages. Hephaestus was able to make beautiful metal objects, such as armor, and he also created humankind.

Apollo was the god of the sun (as was Helios in earlier times) and was also linked with medicine, archery, music, and prophecy. The island of Delos in the Aegean Sea was sacred to Apollo as it was there that his mother, **Leto** (*LAY-toe*), was supposed to have given birth to him and his sister **Artemis** (*AR-tuh-miss*), the goddess of hunting and the moon. Artemis was also connected with childbirth.

Ares (*AIR-eez*) was the god of war, and **Athena** (*Uh-THEE-nuh*) was the goddess of war. Athena was worshipped throughout the Greek world, but was particularly popular in Athens, because she was its patron goddess. Athena was also the patron goddess of arts and crafts, and the goddess of wisdom. She was often pictured either wearing a helmet, spear, and shield, or with an owl, as owls were thought to be very intelligent birds. Instead of being born in the normal way, she was believed to have sprung fully armed from the head of Zeus.

Demeter (*Duy-MEE-ter*) was the goddess of crops and fertility and was a very important goddess at a time when many Greeks made their living from agriculture. Demeter was also associated with the Mysteries,

Apollo was the god of music. In this image from a Greek vase he is seen playing an early type of harp.

This stone statue of Demeter came from Syracuse, the most powerful Greek city in Sicily. Many artists and poets produced works for its citizens.

which were sacred dramas portraying the death and rebirth of corn. These rituals were believed to signify the mystical death and rebirth of the people who were celebrating them.

Dionysus (*Die-oh-NYE-suss*) was the god of wine and drama. He represented the emotional and uncontrolled side of human beings. He was the son of Zeus and a mortal woman called Semele (*SEM-uh-lee*), who died giving birth to him. He was generally shown carrying grapes and a magic stick called a thyrsus (*THIR-sis*).

Greek and Roman Gods

Many of the Greek gods were also worshipped by the Romans, but mostly by different names:

Greek	Roman equivalent
Aphrodite	Venus, the goddess of love
Apollo	Apollo, the god of the sun
Ares	Mars, the god of war
Artemis	Diana, the huntress
Athena	Minerva, the goddess of wisdom
Demeter	Ceres, the goddess of crops
Dionysus	Bacchus, the god of wine
Hades	Pluto, god of the Underworld
Hephaestus	Vulcan, the blacksmith
Hera	Juno, the wife of Jupiter
Hermes	Mercury, messenger of the gods
Hestia	Vesta, the goddess of the hearth
Poseidon	Neptune, the god of the sea
Zeus	Jupiter, the chief god

Athena was the patron goddess of Athens.

Poseidon (*Puh-SY-dun*) was the god of the sea and is often shown holding a trident and accompanied by a fish or a dolphin. He was also the god of earthquakes and horses. If Poseidon became angry with people he might send terrible sea monsters to kill them or to ruin their land.

Hermes (*HER-meez*) was the messenger of the gods and is normally pictured wearing a winged cap and sandals, and carrying a herald's staff with ribbons or serpents hanging down from it. Hermes was the son of Zeus and Maia (*MY-uh*) and was the patron of travelers, traders, and thieves. He led the souls of the dead down to the Underworld and was also associated with fertility.

Hestia (*HESS-tee-uh*) was the goddess of the hearth, where cooking was done, but little is known about her. **Hades** (*HAY-deez*), the god of the Underworld, was an important, but unpopular god. No temples were dedicated to him and Greeks did not expect to receive any help from him. He was the brother of Zeus and Poseidon. His name was also used to refer to the Underworld.

For the ancient Greeks, the Olympian gods were the main gods, but they also believed in many minor gods and goddesses, such as the gods of the winds. There were also other religious figures, such as the Furies, who took revenge on people who killed their relatives, and the nymphs, who were the spirits of nature and lived in woods, caves, and trees.

The Importance of Myth and Religion

Although the Greeks were great thinkers and one of the first peoples to try to provide scientific explanations for why the world was as it was, they did not have a very good understanding of scientific events. Myth was important to them as it provided explanations for natural phenomena. For example, the sea-god, Poseidon, was known as "The Earth-Shaker" and earthquakes were supposed to be caused by Poseidon becoming angry.

Religion was also very important as a form of social control. There were some actions that were outlawed because it was said that the gods did not approve of them. For example, Zeus was the protector of strangers, so it was considered wrong to kill travelers or, in particular, ambassadors. This was a very important belief as it meant that ambassadors could travel from one city-state to another in times of war without the threat of being killed.

Different Roles

Apollo was the god of music and of medicine, but he could also be worshipped as Apollo the Mouse God. Apollo had gained this attribute because mice and rats were the bringers of plague, and so were connected with medicine. To sacrifice to Apollo in his role as the Mouse God was believed to help to prevent infection from disease-carrying rodents.

The Greek Creation Myth

The ancient Greeks believed that at the very beginning of time there was only Gaia (earth) and Uranus (the sky). Uranus sent rain to Gaia and she produced the grass and the trees, the birds and all other creatures. Gaia and Uranus then had children, called the Titans. Eventually, the youngest Titan, Kronos (*KROH-noss*), led the others in overthrowing their father. Kronos then became the ruler of the earth and married Rhea (*REE-uh*).

However, Kronos had been warned that one of his sons would overthrow him, just as he had overthrown his father. Therefore, whenever Rhea had children, Kronos swallowed them. Rhea was very angry about this, and was determined to save at least one child. When Rhea gave birth to Zeus, she wrapped up a stone in swaddling clothes and gave this to Kronos, pretending that it was the newborn baby. Kronos swallowed the stone, thinking that he was swallowing his son. However, Zeus had been safely hidden away and was able to grow to manhood. Then, when he was strong, he fought and overcame his father. Zeus then banished all the Titans from earth and divided the world between himself and his brothers. Zeus became the ruler of the gods, Poseidon had control of the sea, and Hades ruled over the Underworld.

Olympus, the highest mountain in Greece, was believed to be the home of the gods.

Sometimes the gods' disapproval strengthened state law. For example, murder was illegal, but it also angered the gods.

Sacrifice and Ceremony

The ancient Greeks communicated with the gods in a variety of ways about every aspect of human life, including marriage, adoption, crops, trade, and war. Prayers to the gods were very common, but they had to be said in the right way and addressed to the correct god, using as many of his titles as possible. Prayers were often accompanied by a gift of an offering (generally a small statue) or by libations (*lie-BAY-shins*), where wine or water was poured onto the ground. The gods might also be asked to harm enemies. When this happened, curses were written on tablets and dedicated in temples or left in graves.

The best method of getting the gods' help was through animal sacrifice, usually of a sheep or a cow. A priest, wearing a garland, would lead an animal up to an altar. The animal had to

The Parthenon was decorated with a frieze that depicted the great procession in honor of Athena, called the Panathenaia. This drawing shows part of a reconstructed version of the frieze. Men are leading sheep and cattle to be sacrificed, and bringing water. The second row shows women bringing incense. The bottom row shows the gods, and more women presenting a sacred robe that will be draped around the statue of Athena.

be perfectly formed or the gods would be angry. A prayer was recited and holy water was sprinkled on the head of the animal. Sacred grain was then placed on the altar and a lock of hair was cut from the animal and burned. Then the animal would be stunned with a blow from an axe and its throat cut. The blood was collected in a bowl and poured onto the altar. The entrails would be investigated for omens to predict the future, then fat and thigh bones were burned as an offering to the gods. The remainder of the meat would be eaten by those attending the ceremony, and would make a welcome change from the usual diet of cereal or fish.

Healing

Ancient Greeks often asked for the gods' help in medical matters. Clay models of diseased parts of the body were dedicated in temples, either because the sufferer had recovered, or in the hope that the gods would heal them. It was believed that sleeping overnight in a temple could often help illness, because the god might visit and remove the sickness. Infertile women also visited temples and prayed to Hera to help them to have children.

The Greeks believed that if someone had done something wrong, or had been in contact with death or medical matters, then they became polluted. For example, women were considered to remain polluted from childbirth for forty days after the birth. It was necessary to get rid of this pollution to stop it from spreading to other people. Special ceremonies of purification were carried out where prayers were said to make the polluted person clean again.

Religious Festivals and Sites

There were many different festivals held to honor the gods. In Athens there were at least sixty city-state festivals as well as many smaller, local ones. The most important Greek

A reconstruction of the Temple of Artemis at Ephesus. Built on the site of an even earlier shrine to Artemis, this temple was constructed in the fourth century B.C.E. and was one of the Seven Wonders of the Ancient World. At around 170 feet (52 meters) wide and 366 feet (112 meters) long, it was one of the largest buildings ever built at the time.

Temples were decorated with sculpture on the pediment, or triangular front, of the building. Temple decoration was also often painted in bright colors.

The temple stood on top of a set of steps. The steps acted as a protection against flooding.

Temples had grand entrances to make them even more impressive. Statues often lined the steps leading up to the temple.

There were a large number of columns in the temple of Artemis. There was a triple row of eight columns at the front and a double row of twenty-one columns along the sides. The bottom of the columns were covered with carvings.

Temples were part of the everyday life of the Greeks. People would meet and talk outside them.

festivals were the Pythian (*PITH-ee-un*) Games at Delphi and those held at Nemea (*NEE-mee-uh*), Olympia, and Corinth. Major athletic competitions (such as the Olympic Games) would be held at these festivals, as well as competitions in music, poetry, and drama.

The Athenians also held the Panathenaia (*Pa-na-then-EYE-uh*), or "All-Athenian" festival in honor of Athena. This festival included a long procession toward the Acropolis of Athens. Both men and women could take part, and non-citizens and freed slaves were also allowed to attend. Some festivals were reserved for women only, such as the Thesmophoria (*Thez-moe-FOE-ree-uh*) at Athens. Slaves were allowed to take part in the Mysteries at Eleusis (near Athens) and may have shared in some of the festival holidays.

The locations of religious sites varied. Some, such as Delphi, had very dramatic settings in the middle of the mountains, and some were in the center of towns. Hephaestus was a god of craftspeople, so he was normally worshipped in industrial areas. The site might consist of just one temple or a collection of temples, such as on the Acropolis at Athens. The most common building was a temple, but there might also be formal gateways or dining areas.

The Oracle at Delphi

The Greeks liked to be able to find out what was going to happen and believed that highly skilled prophets could predict the future by investigating the entrails of animals, or by watching the flight of birds. However, the best method of predicting the future was to ask an oracle. There were various oracles in the Greek world (such as the one on the island of Delos), but the most famous was at Delphi. Many different questions could be asked, such as whom one should marry, or whether or not a state should go to war. Once the questioner had paid a fee (which increased according to the importance of the question), a priest would ask Apollo, the god of prophecy, for an answer. The answer was spoken by the Pythia (*PITH-ee-uh*), or priestess, who was supposed to be inspired by Apollo. Her reply was then interpreted by priests. The advice was often difficult to understand and so the questioner was blamed for misinterpreting the oracle if things later went wrong.

The Story of Croesus

Not only Greeks, but also foreigners, asked the Delphic oracle for advice. The ruler of Lydia (in modern Turkey), King Croesus (*KREE-suss*), asked the oracle whether he should attack the Persians. He was told that if he attacked the Persians he would destroy a great empire. Croesus thought that this meant that he would defeat the Persians, but when he went to war, it was he who was defeated. The oracle had come true, but it was his own empire that had been destroyed.

A marble head of Zeus dating from the second century B.C.E. Zeus was the greatest of the Olympian gods and was known to the Romans as Jupiter.

Chapter Two

The Trojan War

The ancient Greeks believed that long ago there had been a great war between them and the Trojans, who lived in Troy (in what is now Turkey). The war happened partly due to the gods and partly due to the actions of one man, Paris.

The Start of the Trojan War

The gods had gathered together to celebrate the marriage of King Peleus (*Puh-LAY-us*) to the sea-nymph Thetis. Everyone had been invited except bad-tempered Eris (*EH-riss*), the goddess of discord. When she discovered that the gods were holding a feast without her she planned her revenge. She entered the hall and flung down a beautiful golden apple, which had the words "For the fairest" inscribed on it. Naturally, all the goddesses wanted to be called the most beautiful, and so all claimed the prize as their own. One by one they dropped out of the contest until only Hera, Athena, and Aphrodite were left. Nobody wanted to choose which goddess was the most beautiful, as they knew that the two goddesses who did not win would be extremely angry with the judge. Therefore Zeus decided to ask Paris, the son of the king and queen of Troy, to decide the contest.

The messenger god, Hermes, was sent to Troy, and ordered Paris to choose between the three goddesses. Next the goddesses came. Each was determined to win, and each offered Paris a bribe to encourage him to choose her. Athena said that he would have

The Trojans thought that the Wooden Horse of Troy had been left as an offering to Athena by the Greeks. However, it was part of a cunning plan by Odysseus to help the Greeks to capture the city.

Greek pots often showed scenes from mythology. The inside of this drinking cup shows Athena seated holding a helmet and spear.

great wisdom if he chose her, while Hera promised that he would have great wealth and tremendous power if she were crowned the fairest. Finally, Aphrodite, the goddess of love, appeared and promised Paris the most beautiful woman in the world as his wife if he chose her. Paris decided in Aphrodite's favor, greatly angering the other two goddesses.

With the help of Aphrodite, Paris then sailed to Greece in order to acquire the most beautiful woman in the world, Helen. At this time Helen was living in Sparta where she was married to the king, Menelaus (*Men-uh-LAY-us*). When Paris arrived at Sparta he was welcomed and treated very well by Menelaus and Helen. However, he treacherously repaid this hospitality by abducting Helen and sailing back to Troy. When Menelaus discovered what had happened he was furious and called on his older brother, Agamemnon (*A-guh-MEM-non*), the king of Mycenae (*My-SEE-nigh*), to help him to recover Helen and punish Paris.

The Sacrifice of Iphigenia

A great army of warriors came from across Greece and gathered together at Aulis (*OW-liss*), in central Greece. All the men and ships were ready, but they were unable to leave the harbor because the winds were unfavorable and prevented them from sailing. Day after day they waited in the harbor, expecting the winds to change so that they would be able to sail to Troy. However, no favorable winds came and, eventually, the Greeks asked Calchas (*KAL-kuss*) what was wrong. Calchas was the soothsayer, or prophet, of the army and he was able to predict the future as well as to discover the wishes of the gods.

Calchas said that the army was unable to sail because of the anger of the gods. Agamemnon, the leader of the army, had boasted that he was a greater hunter than Artemis. She demanded that he pay a dreadful price for his arrogance; he must kill his own daughter Iphigenia (*If-uh-JEN-eye-uh*) or the ships would be unable to leave port. Agamemnon was very unhappy when he learned this news and he tried to appease the goddess with other costly sacrifices. However, the

This first-century B.C.E. Roman mosaic from the ruins of Ampurias, Spain, shows Agamemnon preparing to sacrifice his daughter, Iphigenia. Her death would ensure that the Greek fleet could sail to Troy.

goddess remained angry and the ships remained in the harbor. Eventually, the other Greeks threatened to return to Greece if Agamemnon would not obey Artemis' command. Realizing that there would be no war with Troy if he did not sacrifice Iphigenia, Agamemnon gave in. He sent a messenger to Sparta demanding that Iphigenia be brought to Aulis.

Agamemnon knew that his wife Clytemnestra (*Kly-tem-NESS-truh*) would never bring her daughter to Aulis if she learned what he planned to do. Therefore he told her that the great hero Achilles (*Uh-KILL-eez*) wanted to marry Iphigenia before the ships set sail for Troy. Clytemnestra was very pleased at the prospect of her daughter becoming the wife of one of the most important Greeks and she left Mycenae as quickly as possible. However, when she arrived at Aulis she discovered the truth: she had brought her daughter to her death. Clytemnestra begged Agamemnon to reconsider his decision, but in vain. Achilles, the great hero who was supposedly going to marry Iphigenia, also refused to help. Finally, Iphigenia told her mother that she was willing to die to help the Greeks and she very bravely went to her death. Tradition records that the goddess

The gold death-mask of a Mycenaean king. When the first excavator of Mycenae, Heinrich Schliemann, discovered this mask he believed that he had "gazed upon the face of Agamemnon." However, the mask dates to before the time of the Trojan War.

The Death of Iphigenia

The great Greek playwright Euripides (*You-RIP-i-deez*) wrote two plays about Iphigenia. In one of them, *Iphigenia in Aulis*, the young girl speaks of her love for Greece and her desire to help the Greeks by dying nobly and willingly for them:

Mother, hear what I have decided to do. I am ready to die. I want to act nobly and not in a shameful way. All of mighty Greece now looks to me. The sailing of our ships depends upon me. The destruction of the Trojans depends upon me. The protection of our women depends upon me. When Paris has paid the price for the abduction of Helen, barbarians shall never again be allowed to seize our women. I shall ensure all of these things by dying and I shall be famous as the woman who set Greece free. It is not right for me to love life too much, for you did not give birth to me just for yourself, but as the common possession of all of Greece.

Euripides, *Iphigenia in Aulis*

Artemis snatched her up from the sacrificial altar at the last moment and put a deer down in her place. However, Clytemnestra was left very bitter and angry at the betrayal of her daughter and she vowed to take revenge on Agamemnon.

Achilles and Patroclus

When fighting took place any male captives tended to be killed, but female captives were enslaved. The Greek troops had captured Chryseis (*Kry-SAYSS*), who was the daughter of a priest of Apollo called Chryses (*KRY-seez*). Agamemnon, as the chief commander, had demanded Chryseis as his own slave. When Chryses learned what had happened to his daughter, he hurried to Agamemnon's tent and begged him to release her. Agamemnon laughed at him and refused to accept the ransom he was offered. However, Chryses was wise in the ways of his master, Apollo, and begged him to curse the Greeks. Apollo heard his prayer and sent a dreadful plague into the camp. Soon the Greeks were dying in large numbers and nobody knew how to halt the disease. Again the Greeks turned to the soothsayer Calchas, who instructed them that the only way to avert the disease was to appease Apollo's anger and return Chryseis to her grieving father. Agamemnon agreed that he would do this, but demanded that he receive another beautiful captive, Briseis (*Bry-SAYSS*), in return.

Briseis belonged to Achilles and he was very angry that Agamemnon was demanding his captive. He let Agamemnon take Briseis only because he did not want the Greeks to continue to suffer from the plague. However, he said that he would no longer fight for Agamemnon because he could not follow a commander who treated him so poorly. Achilles was the best of the Greek warriors, so his absence soon became noticed; the Greeks fought less well and the Trojans

Homer and the War at Troy

The *Iliad* (*ILL-ee-ad*) tells the story of the war at Troy. The Greeks believed that it was written by a blind poet called Homer, who also wrote the *Odyssey* (*ODD-iss-ee*), which tells the adventures of Odysseus (*Oh-DISS-ee-us*) on his way home from Troy.

Today we are not sure whether the same poet wrote the two books, or whether there were many tales handed down over time and finally compiled into two books. A very important part of the *Iliad* focuses on the quarrel between the great hero Achilles and Agamemnon, the leader of the Greek forces.

gained strength. The other Greeks begged Achilles to help them but he refused. Even his best friend, Patroclus (*Puh-TRO-kluss*), could not persuade him to change his mind.

Patroclus now put into action a clever plan to improve the morale of the Greeks. He asked Achilles to lend him his armor and went into battle disguised as his friend. The Trojans, thinking that the most feared Greek warrior was returning, lost heart and started to retreat. Then Hector, the son of the Trojan King Priam (*PRY-um*), challenged Patroclus to a fight. They fought ferociously for a long time until finally Hector overcame Patroclus. The deception was revealed; it was Patroclus, not Achilles, who lay dead in the dust. Achilles wept with anger and grief when he learned of the death of his friend and vowed to avenge him. The next day, Achilles set out from camp seeking Hector. At first Hector tried to flee, but then he turned and fought Achilles. However, Achilles soon defeated him and, still raging at the death of Patroclus, he achieved his revenge. Tying Hector's body to his chariot, Achilles drove around the walls of Troy with the body dragging in the dust behind him.

Every day Achilles dragged Hector's body around the walls of Troy, to the great grief of Hector's parents, Hecuba (*HEH-kew-buh*) and Priam, and his wife, Andromache (*An-dro-MAH-kee*). Eventually the gods grew angry with Achilles' actions,

The Greek soldiers made many daring attempts to capture Troy, including attempting to scale the city walls, but the war lasted for ten years.

The Death of Hector

The story of the death of Hector is told in the *Iliad*, the first account of the Trojan War.

Achilles attacked, with savage anger filling his heart. He thrust his sharp spear into Hector's soft neck and he crashed to the dust. Then god-like Achilles boasted to him: "Hector, when you killed Patroclus you thought that you would be safe and you did not fear me because I was far off. But the dogs and vultures will maul your body vilely."

Then Hector of the gleaming helmet answered with the remains of his strength, "I beg you by your life and by your parents, do not let the dogs feed on me, but take the ransom of bronze and gold which my father will give you and send my body back home so that I can be buried in the proper way."

Swift-footed Achilles looked sternly at him and retorted, "You dog, do not beseech me in the name of your parents! I wish that I could hack away and eat your flesh myself, considering what you have done to me. Nobody is going to keep the dogs away from your head, even if they bring ten or twenty times your ransom, even if Priam offers your weight in gold."

Then the final act of death covered Hector and his spirit fled from his limbs and went to Hades, lamenting its fate.

Homer, *Iliad*

This fifth-century B.C.E. vase shows the death of Patroclus. Achilles was so shocked at his friend's death that he returned to fight for the Greeks.

An Achilles Heel

One of the reasons for Achilles' greatness as a warrior was that his mother, Thetis, had dipped him in the river Styx (*Sticks*), in the Underworld, when he was a baby. Whichever section of a mortal's body touched the river could no longer be wounded. The only part of Achilles' body that had not been immersed in the Styx was the heel by which Thetis had held him. Achilles was practically invulnerable in combat, but he did have one place where he could be harmed. This is the origin of the saying "an Achilles heel," which refers to a person's weak spot.

Thetis holds Achilles by his heel and dips him into the waters of the river Styx.

and his mother, Thetis, ordered him to let King Priam ransom his son's body. Achilles gave in, and Hector's body was brought back to Troy for burial. Shortly afterward Achilles was killed by Paris, who shot him with an arrow in the one spot where he was vulnerable, his heel. Paris himself was struck down by a poisoned arrow and died in agony.

Achilles had only one weak spot in his body, his heel. Paris shot an arrow into his heel and killed him.

The Trojan Horse

The Trojan War had now been going on for ten years and the Greeks despaired of ever capturing the city. It was at this point that Odysseus, the most cunning of the Greeks, proposed that since they had failed to take the city by force of arms, they ought to try to capture it by trickery. The Greeks agreed with him and decided to carry out his plan. A giant horse was built out of wood and in the hollow center the bravest of the Greeks hid themselves. Then the rest of the Greek army pretended that they were tired of battle and went to their ships. The ships sailed away, leaving the wooden horse standing alone on the shore.

When the Trojans came out of the city the next day they looked in amazement at the remains of the Greek camp. When they finally gained the courage to investigate the shore they discovered no sign of the Greeks, only the huge wooden horse. At this point a search party returned, with a captive Greek. This man, called Sinon (*SIGH-non*), pretended that he had deserted from the Greek army because Odysseus had said that he was going to kill him. Sinon claimed that the wooden horse was an offering to Athena from the Greeks. Some of the Trojans therefore wanted to destroy the horse, but Sinon said that if they did that, Athena would be angry with them. However, if they brought the horse into the city, they would be able to invade Greece.

Laocoon and the Sea Snakes

Laocoon (*Lay-OCK-oh-on*), the priest of Poseidon, tried to persuade the Trojans not to bring the horse into the city. "Trojans," he warned, "do you not know Odysseus better than this? Do not trust this horse. I fear the Greeks, even when they bring gifts!" He then struck the side of the horse with his spear to show that it was hollow. The Trojans were partly persuaded by his words, but then two huge sea snakes swam toward him, came

Laocoon warned the Trojans not to trust the Wooden Horse. He was punished by the gods who sent two giant sea snakes that killed him and his sons.

The Fate of the Trojans

Only a few of the Trojans managed to escape from Troy. One of these was Aeneas (*Ee-NEE-us*) who, after many adventures, managed to sail to Italy and found a new homeland there for the Trojans. The ancient Romans were very interested in the story of the Trojan War because they believed that they were descended from Aeneas. The journey of Aeneas from Troy to Italy is recounted in a famous epic written by the Roman poet Virgil, called the *Aeneid*.

The Fall of Troy **by the seventeenth-century artist Jean Maublanc. The Wooden Horse is at the bottom right.**

out of the sea, and crushed him and his two young sons to death. The Trojans thought that this was a sign that the gods were angry with Laocoon for trying to persuade them to destroy the horse, and they were fearful of further angering the gods. So, with great rejoicing, they brought the horse into the city. At night, while the Trojans were feasting and celebrating the end of the war, Sinon slipped off to the horse and let out the warriors. They made their way to the gates of Troy and opened them. Now the other Greeks, who had secretly sailed back to Troy, entered the city and captured it.

When the Greeks entered Troy they showed no mercy. A few Trojans escaped the carnage and fled from the city, but the Greeks were intent on revenge. They sacked the city and slaughtered most of the people they found. Those who were not killed were enslaved. Neither the old nor the noble were spared. King Priam was cut down while praying at an altar, Hector's wife Andromache was taken as a slave, and his baby son Astyanax (*Ast-EYE-an-ax*) was killed. There was violence and destruction throughout the city. The temples were pillaged of their precious offerings and then

A brutal fate awaited Agamemnon when he returned home, as this second-century B.C.E carving shows.

set on fire; the houses were ransacked and destroyed. Only when the whole city lay in ruins and its inhabitants were dead or captured did the Greeks set sail from Troy, with their ships full of loot and captives.

The Fate of Agamemnon

When Menelaus finally entered Troy, he fully intended to kill his wife Helen if he found her. However, when he caught sight of her he was overcome with love and spared her life. They returned to Sparta and lived happily together for many years. His brother Agamemnon was not so fortunate when he returned home.

Agamemnon returned in triumph to Mycenae, laden with loot and slaves, including Cassandra, the daughter of King Priam. However, Agamemnon had been away from Mycenae for ten years and in that time his wife Clytemnestra had fallen in love with his cousin, Aegisthus (*Eye-GISS-thuss*). She had never forgiven Agamemnon for betraying their daughter, Iphigenia, and she did not wish to be his wife any more. She was also greatly enraged that he had brought Cassandra to Greece. Aegisthus also did not like Agamemnon because Agamemnon's father had cheated his father out of becoming the ruler of Mycenae. Aegisthus had been acting as king in Agamemnon's absence and he had no intention of giving up his power. Thus Clytemnestra and Aegisthus planned to kill Agamemnon and rule as king and queen of Mycenae.

A Cursed Family

The Greeks believed that one of the reasons that events turned out poorly for Agamemnon was because of the lack of respect for the gods shown by his ancestors. His great-grandfather, Tantalus (*TAN-tuh-luss*), had been a friend of the gods until he decided to test their intelligence. He killed his own son Pelops (*PAY-lops*) and served up his body at a feast, where Demeter ate part of his flesh.

The gods took pity on Pelops, restored him to life, and gave him an ivory shoulder in place of the flesh that Demeter had eaten. Tantalus was immortal, so the gods punished him by sending him to Tartarus, where he had to stand in flowing water with fruit-laden trees above his head. Whenever he tried to drink, the water level dropped below his reach, and whenever he tried to pluck the fruit, the branches were blown away from him. Thus Tantalus was condemned to suffer eternal punishment.

The legend of Tantalus is the origin of the word "tantalize," meaning to tease someone with the sight or promise of something unobtainable.

Deceived by His Wife

Clytemnestra pretended that she was delighted to see her husband and led him to the bath-house, where a warm bath was waiting for him. Agamemnon was tired after his journey back from Troy and was happy to relax in a bath. When he emerged from the water, intending to get ready for the great feast which was to be held in his honor, Clytemnestra approached him. Agamemnon thought that she had brought him a towel to dry himself, but instead Clytemnestra flung a net over him. As Agamemnon struggled to escape, Aegisthus struck him with a sword. Agamemnon fell back into the bath, where Clytemnestra finished him off with an axe.

Clytemnestra then killed Cassandra while Aegisthus overcame Agamemnon's bodyguard. Aegisthus wanted to also kill Agamemnon's son, Orestes (*Or-ESS-teez*), but his older sister Electra (*Uh-LEK-truh*) managed to lead him to safety. They took shelter with the King of Phocis (*FO-kiss*) and stayed there for several years. Then, when Orestes was a young man, they made their way back to Mycenae where Orestes killed his mother Clytemnestra and Aegisthus.

Fact or Fiction: Was There a Trojan War?

The Trojan War has such a key role in the Greek myths that for centuries the Greeks thought it must have taken place. Today we think rather differently. We do not believe that gods and goddesses took part in a war, nor do we believe that all the heroes really existed. However, while many of those who were supposed to take part in the war were almost certainly mythical, archaeological evidence suggests that there is some truth behind the legend. Sparta, Mycenae, Troy, and other places mentioned by Homer certainly existed, although Mycenae's period of greatest power is much earlier than Homer thought. There are signs of conflict in the region of Troy, and the city was certainly destroyed at one point in a war. Many of the details given in Homer relate to the eighth century B.C.E., rather than the thirteenth century B.C.E., when the Trojan War took place. For example, Homer often describes bodies being cremated, whereas this was very rare in Mycenaean times, when bodies were usually buried in graves. Moreover, modern archaeologists believe that any war between Greeks and Trojans would have happened because of quarrels over trade, not because a woman had been abducted!

The ruins of Troy today. Little is left of a once-great city.

Chapter Three

The Wanderings of Odysseus

The Greeks were seafarers and traveled all around the Mediterranean and beyond. Therefore it was natural for them to tell tales about exotic creatures and outlandish places, which reflected the perils of exploring the waves in small ships. Many of these stories were attached to the mythical figure of Odysseus, who was supposed to have spent ten years sailing the seas in a desperate attempt to return home from the Trojan War. Odysseus was a typical "folk hero"—a man who shows considerable cunning and survives against all the odds.

Adventures with the Lotus-Eaters

As the Greek ships were sailing west from Troy, a dreadful storm blew up. For ten days Odysseus and his companions were buffeted by gales. Eventually, blown far off course, they arrived at the land of the Lotus-Eaters. Odysseus sent three men inland to search for food and water. After they had been gone a long time, Odysseus feared that something had happened to them and set out to find them. When he did, he saw that they had not been captured by angry locals. Rather, they had been treated with kindness and fed lotus fruit and lotus blossoms. The problem was that whoever ate the food of the lotus plant immediately forgot who they were and where they lived. They no longer wanted to go home, but rather wished to stay and eat lotus fruit forever.

The mythical hero Odysseus spent ten years trying to return home to his family in Ithaca after the end of the Trojan War. Greek ships were small and sailing in rough seas was difficult and dangerous.

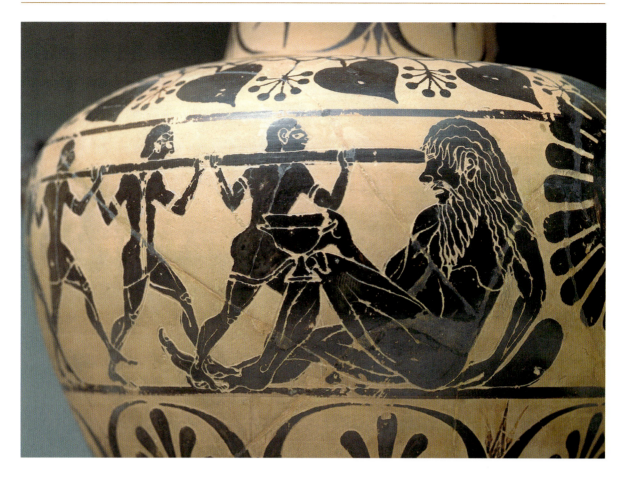

This fifth-century B.C.E. vase shows the blinding of the cyclops, Polyphemus. Odysseus and his sailors drive a sharp wooden stake into Polyphemus' single eye.

Odysseus ordered his companions not to eat any of the fruit, and they seized the three men. Protesting, they were dragged back to the ships and forced to embark. Finally, as they sailed far away from the land of the Lotus-Eaters, the drugged men returned to their senses and remembered who they were.

Polyphemus the Cyclops

Shortly after this, the ships arrived at Sicily. Odysseus and twelve comrades set off to look for food and water. When they found a large cave containing milk and cheese the Greeks waited to ask the owner of the food if they might have some. However, when the owner returned they soon realized that he was not a friendly farmer, but a cyclops (*SIGH-klops*), a terrible giant with only one eye in the middle of his forehead. The Greeks tried to hide but the cyclops, Polyphemus (*Poll-uh-FEE-muss*), soon found them and asked them who they were. Odysseus said that they were Greeks returning home from war and claimed the protection of Zeus, who cared for travelers. Polyphemus laughed and said that he was more important than the gods. Then he snatched two of the men, threw them to the rocky floor, and ate them.

The Greeks were unable to escape because Polyphemus had blocked the entrance to the cave with a huge boulder, which they could not move. The next day the cyclops ate two more men and then left to look after his sheep. While he was away, the remaining Greeks made a great wooden stake and hardened its point in the fire.

When the cyclops returned Odysseus gave him some wine. Polyphemus thanked him and asked him his name, promising that he would eat him last of all. Odysseus lied, and said that he was called "Nobody." Soon the wine made the cyclops sleepy. While he slept, the Greeks picked up the wooden stake and drove it into his eye. Polyphemus awoke, screaming in agony and blind. Other cyclopes (*sigh-CLOE-peez*) came running to ask what was wrong, but he cried out that "Nobody" was hurting him. They could not understand what he was shouting about and left him, not realizing that there were men in the cave harming one of their friends.

The next morning, Odysseus tied his men underneath the cyclops' giant sheep, and he himself clung on to the belly of the great ram of the flock. As the cyclops let his sheep out to graze, the Greeks escaped. However, once they had reached their ship and were sailing away, Odysseus foolishly called out who he really was. Polyphemus then knew who had hurt him and he begged his father, Poseidon, to punish the man who had blinded him.

A sculpture of the head of Odysseus dating from the second century B.C.E. This is believed to be a copy of an even earlier Greek statue.

Aeolus, the Ruler of the Winds

Shocked by their deadly encounter with Polyphemus, the Greeks were even more eager than ever to return home. Now they came to the island where Aeolus (*EE-oh-luss*), the king of the winds, lived. Aeolus treated the Greeks well while they rested on his island. When they were ready to depart, Aeolus gave Odysseus a leather sack containing all the winds except one. The one wind that was not tied up was the wind that would blow them in the right direction.

However, Odysseus had not told the sailors what was in the bag and they were jealous because they thought that Aeolus had given Odysseus great riches, that he was not going to share with them. Therefore, while he slept, they opened the bag to look for the treasures inside. Out rushed all of the winds with a great roar and Odysseus woke up to see the ships being blown off their homeward course. Although they returned to the Isle of Aeolus, the king was angry with them and refused to help them a second time.

The Laestrygonians

The cyclops Polyphemus was not the only man-eater Odysseus met. After the Greeks left Aeolus for the second time, they reached the land of the Laestrygonians (*Lye-stri-GO-nee-ans*). The Laestrygonians were giant man-eaters who ate anyone who landed on their territory. They threw rocks at Odysseus' ships, sinking several of them and eating the crews.

The Enchantress Circe

Shortly afterward, Odysseus came to the island of the enchantress Circe (*SIR-see*). One group of men went inland to explore and soon came to a palace set in a clearing in a forest. There they saw many wild animals behaving in a very tame manner. Then a beautiful woman emerged from the palace and asked them to enter and take refreshment with her. All of the men except one, called Eurylochus (*You-RILL-oh-kuss*), did so. Eurylochus was frightened and waited outside. Then, to his horror, he saw that his friends turned into pigs when they ate the food that Circe had given them. Eurylochus rushed back to tell Odysseus the dreadful news. Odysseus set off at once to rescue his unfortunate companions. As he was hurrying through the forest the god Hermes appeared in front of him and gave him a magic flower called moly (*MOE-lee*). Hermes told him that the moly would protect him from Circe's spells. Just as Hermes had promised, when Circe tried to turn him into an animal, the flower protected Odysseus and Circe realized that he had the protection of the gods. Odysseus forced Circe to turn all the animals back into human beings and so saved his men from a dreadful fate.

When Circe gave Odysseus' men a special potion they were turned into pigs. This vase painting dates from around 500–475 B.C.E.

A Visit to the Underworld

After Odysseus had defeated Circe's spells, she gave a splendid banquet for all of the men she had bewitched. Odysseus and his men remained with her for a year and then decided to set off homeward again. Circe warned him that his journey would be difficult and that he ought to visit the Underworld to ask advice from the seer, Tiresias (*Ty-REE-see-us*). Odysseus obeyed Circe's instructions, despite considerable fear of the consequences. By the river Acheron (*AK-uh-ron*) he sacrificed a ram and a black ewe to Hades and Persephone. All of a sudden shades (or ghosts) of the dead appeared, eager to drink the warm blood. Odysseus held them back until Tiresias appeared. The seer explained that Odysseus faced many dangers because Poseidon had not forgiven him for blinding his son, the cyclops Polyphemus. Tiresias advised Odysseus that if he made a sacrifice to Poseidon, he would eventually reach home.

The Sirens

Odysseus now organized his men to set sail. Before he left, Circe warned him about the Sirens. These were creatures with the faces of beautiful girls and the bodies of birds. Although they could no longer fly to catch their prey, they were still able to destroy men by singing such bewitching songs from their island that sailors forgot what they were doing and sailed their ships onto the rocks beneath. Circe told Odysseus that if he and his men blocked up their ears with beeswax they would not hear the Sirens' songs and would be able to escape.

Odysseus very much wanted to hear the beautiful songs of the Sirens so, although he ordered his sailors to block up their ears, he did not block up his own. Instead, he had his men tie him to the mast of the ship so that he was able to listen to the songs. Odysseus was enraptured by

Odysseus Meets the Ghost of His Mother

Odysseus traveled to the Underworld in order to consult the prophet Tiresias, but he also met many other ghosts, including his mother. In this extract he tells what happened:

After Tiresias' ghost retreated to the house of Hades, I waited until my mother came toward the blood and drank it. Then she knew that I was her son and she spoke words of grief: 'How can you have entered this dark, misty land, although you are still alive? Have you left Troy only now?'

I was desperate to hold her close. I leaped forward three times, but three times she slipped through my arms like a shadow of a dream. My heart was wounded with bitter pain, for I longed to hold her and weep together with her.

Homer, *Odyssey*

Odysseus learned then that the dead had no shape and could no longer embrace or be embraced. After Odysseus' mother gave him news about his wife and son, he was forced to depart, unable to take his mother with him.

the Sirens' singing and ranted and raved at his men to untie him and let him throw himself to his doom, but the sailors ignored him and sailed the ship out of earshot. Only then was Odysseus released, safe and unharmed.

Scylla and Charybdis

The next dangers facing the Greeks were the giant whirlpool, Charybdis (*Ka-RIB-diss*), and the monster Scylla (*SILL-uh*), who had six heads and twelve feet. These dangers lay so close together that it was extremely difficult not to sail into the clutches of one or the other. Although Odysseus managed to escape Charybdis completely, the ship sailed too close to Scylla. The monster snatched six of his men and ate them alive.

The Cattle of Helios

The seer, Tiresias, had warned Odysseus that, if he were to land on the island of Trinacria (*Tree-NAY-kree-uh*), where Helios, the god of the sun, kept his cattle, he must on no account harm the animals. When the ship sailed near to the island of Trinacria the men begged to go ashore and rest. Odysseus feared that they might harm the god's cattle, but the men

The Sirens lured sailors to their doom, but Odysseus, determined to hear their bewitching song, had himself tied to the mast of his ship.

The monster Scylla lived on a cliff and lay in wait for passing ships. She had six heads, each of which had long necks. She was able to reach down from the top of the cliff and snatch sailors from their vessels.

SCYLLA

Odysseus had to sail close to the cliff where Scylla lived in order to avoid being sucked into the whirlpool, Charybdis.

ODYSSEUS' SHIP

promised that they would not do so. Unfortunately, when they had landed and rested they could not leave the island as the winds prevented them from setting sail. The men had very little food and grew desperate. Finally they killed some of the cattle. Helios was furious and told the other gods that he would no longer shine upon the earth if the offenders were not punished. The gods agreed to act and, when the sailors set sail, there came a dreadful storm. All except Odysseus, who had not eaten the sacred meat, perished in the waves.

Charybdis was a giant whirlpool. Odysseus knew that many sailors had drowned when they sailed too close to Charybdis.

STEEP CLIFFS

CHARYBDIS

Calypso and Nausicaa

Odysseus clung onto a piece of wood from the broken ship until he was blown to the island of the nymph Calypso (*Kuh-LIP-so*). He had to remain there for many years, because no ships ever visited the island and he had no means of escape. Eventually Zeus ordered that Calypso must provide Odysseus with the materials to make a giant raft, and let him sail away.

Odysseus soon built his raft, but Poseidon still hated Odysseus and wished to kill him. He sent a huge wave, which swept Odysseus off his raft. Odysseus managed to swim to the land of the Phaeacians (*Fee-AY-shuns*). There he was found by the princess Nausicaa (*Now-SIK-ah-ah*) who took him to the palace. Her father, King Alcinous (*Al-kin-OH-uss*), was amazed when he learned that the famous Odysseus had come to his shores. He looked after him well and then sent him back to his home on Ithaca (believed to have been the island of Corfu).

The Return to Ithaca

Odysseus knew that there must have been many changes at Ithaca since he had last been there. Therefore, he decided to approach the palace disguised as a beggar. He had learned from his loyal swineherd (or pig-keeper), Eumaeus (*You-MAY-us*), that his wife Penelope and his son Telemachus (*Tuh-LEM-uh-kuss*) were alive, but in trouble.

Odysseus and Penelope Reunited

Many men had wanted to marry Penelope after Odysseus had left, but she had refused every single man. Soon they had insisted that she must choose one of them. Penelope promised that she would do so when she had finished weaving a large tapestry. Every night she unpicked what she had woven during the day and thus delayed having to make her choice.

However, the suitors for her hand in marriage discovered her trick and ordered her to finish the tapestry and then choose one of them. Penelope replied that she would marry the man who could do what her husband Odysseus had once done. This was to string his giant war bow and to shoot an arrow through the rings of twelve axe-handles placed in a row. Very few of the men could even bend the great bow, let alone string it. Then Odysseus stood up and demanded that he should also attempt to carry out the task. All the suitors laughed at the idea of a beggar doing what they could not do. Yet Odysseus not only managed to string the bow, but also shot the arrow through the twelve axe-rings at the first attempt.

Now the suitors were frightened, as they realized who the beggar must be. However, they had little time to be afraid, for Odysseus, helped by Telemachus and Eumaeus, seized more arrows and shot them down one by one. At last Odysseus was reunited with his son and his faithful wife Penelope.

Penelope: The Ideal Wife

In Greek myths, men have most of the lead roles. When women do appear, they are often dangerous or evil (such as Circe). Penelope is unusual in both having an important role and being a good woman. She illustrated many of the virtues that the ancient Greeks believed women should show. She was very loyal to her husband, she loved her son, she was skilled in the womanly arts of weaving and sewing, and she was also prepared to use her intelligence to try to keep her family together.

Penelope, the perfect wife, as imagined by a nineteenth-century artist.

The suitors watch in amazement as the disguised Odysseus shoots an arrow through the axe rings.

Chapter Four

Great Quests

Jason and the Argonauts

One popular myth, which reflected the Greeks' interest in trade, was the story of Jason and his search for the Golden Fleece. Jason was supposed to have sailed to Colchis (*KOL-kiss*), in the Black Sea region near the Ukraine, to find the fleece. The Greeks believed that the East was a land of mystery, intrigue, and great wealth. In particular, the figure of the witch, Medea (*Muh-DEE-uh*), reflected the belief that sorcery and magic were common in that part of the world. The Greeks were both fascinated with, and wary of, people who had very different customs from their own.

Jason was the son of Aeson (*A-EE-sun*). Aeson ought to have been the king of Iolcos (*Ee-OLE-koss*) in Thessaly in northern Greece. However, Aeson's brother Pelias (*Puh-LEE-ass*) had seized the kingdom from Aeson and sent him into exile. Aeson handed Jason over to be brought up by the centaur Chiron (*KI-ron*) because he feared that Pelias would kill the boy. The centaur taught Jason to be brave and noble. When he grew up he wanted to recover his kingdom, and set off to Iolcos. Pelias recognized him and was determined to get rid of him.

Pelias did not want to kill Jason openly, as he feared that to do so would make him unpopular. Instead he laid a cunning trap. A bard (or folksinger) was ordered to sing about the Golden Fleece, which King Aeetes (*Ay-EE-teez*) of Colchis owned. After the

After beheading Medusa, Perseus holds up her head in triumph. This bronze statue was made by the Italian sculptor Cellini in 1553. Note how Perseus is shown wearing the helmet that made him invisible.

An eighteenth-century depiction by the French painter Jean François de Troy (1679–1752) of Jason winning the Golden Fleece, helped by Medea and the Argonauts.

song was over, Pelias spoke of his regret that he was too old to try to win the fleece and said that young men now were too cowardly to attempt such a task. Jason was angry that his courage was in question, and promised that he would win the fleece and return in triumph.

Jason and Medea

Jason now gathered together a crew of heroes, many of whom also had been educated by Chiron. They built a swift ship, called the *Argo* (*AR-go*), and the sailors were called the Argonauts (*AR-go-noughts*). They had many exciting adventures on the way to Colchis, but eventually they arrived at the court of King Aeetes. At first the king received them in a friendly manner, but he became furious when he discovered that the Argonauts intended to seize the Golden Fleece. He therefore set Jason various tasks that he hoped would prove to be impossible.

Jason was ordered to tame two wild, fire-breathing bulls with bronze hooves and horns. Then he was to harness them to a stone plow, with which he was to plow a large field. In the field, he had to sow dragon's teeth as a kind of seed. From this, armed men would spring out of the ground. Jason would have to fight and kill these warriors. Having achieved this, Jason would have the chance to seize the Golden Fleece from the dragon that guarded it and never slept. All this was to be achieved in a single day.

Jason could never have managed these tasks without the help of the king's daughter, Medea, who was skilled in the arts of sorcery. Medea had fallen in love with Jason and offered to help him if he would marry her. Jason eagerly promised to do so, and she gave him potions to tame the bulls and make the dragon fall asleep. Jason also followed Medea's advice to throw a stone into the middle of the armed men that had sprung from the dragon's teeth. Unable to tell where the stone had come from, and confused by the attack, they fought each other.

The Return Home

Jason obeyed Medea's instructions and was able to seize the Golden Fleece. He then sailed away with Medea and her little brother, Absyrtus (*Ab-SIR-tuss*). King Aeetes was very angry and set off in pursuit of the *Argo*. Medea, seeing her father catching up with the ship, decided to distract him. She grabbed hold of Absyrtus and threw him into the sea. Aeetes naturally stopped to collect his son, and the Argonauts were able to sail back to Greece. Jason returned to Iolcos and sent Pelias into exile. Aeson was restored to his rightful position as king, and Jason and Medea had two children.

This fifth-century B.C.E. vase shows the witch Medea escaping in a chariot drawn by dragons after killing her two children.

Is There Any Truth in the Story of the Golden Fleece?

Today, we do not believe that a sheep could have a fleece made of gold. However, there are some parts of Asia where gold particles are found in rivers. One method of obtaining this gold is to put a sheep's fleece into the river and let the water wash over it. When the fleece is removed, any gold particles in the water will stick to the wool and can then be plucked off. It is thought that tales brought back by Greek traders about this custom may have led to the story of the Golden Fleece.

Eventually, Jason fell out of love with Medea and took a new lover. Medea then enacted a terrible revenge. She gave Jason's lover a poisoned robe that killed her when she put it on. Then Medea killed her own children in front of Jason. Finally, she left Iolcos, never to return. Jason died a sad and lonely man.

Perseus and the Gorgon

Even though the story of Perseus (*Per-SEE-uss*) is mythical, it reveals an important aspect of the Greek outlook on life. The tale illustrates the impossibility of mortals escaping the fate that the gods had decreed that they would suffer.

The Birth of Perseus

Acrisius (*Uh-KRIZ-ee-uss*), the king of Argos, was warned by an oracle that his grandson

Danae and her baby Perseus are placed in a wooden chest and sent out to sea. No one thought that they would survive this ordeal.

would kill him, so he decided that his only child, Danae (*Dun-EYE*), must never marry, or even meet any men. Acrisius built a tower of bronze and locked Danae in it, never allowing her to go outside or to be with other people. However, Zeus, the ruler of the gods, felt sorry for Danae and visited her in the shape of a shower of gold. He visited Danae many times. Eventually, they fell in love and Danae became pregnant.

Nine months later, the guards reported to Acrisius that Danae had given birth to a baby boy. Acrisius was extremely angry and vowed that both mother and baby must die. However, he did not want to be directly responsible for their deaths, so he ordered them to be locked in a wooden chest and thrown into the sea. The chest washed ashore on the island of Seriphus (*SIR-ee-fuss*), in the Aegean Sea, and both Danae and her son, Perseus, emerged safely. The king of the island was a man called Polydectes (*Polly-DECK-teez*) and, in the beginning, he treated Danae and Perseus well. After some years, he fell in love with Danae and wished to marry her. However, Danae did not love him and refused to marry him. Perseus proclaimed that nobody would compel his mother to marry someone she did not love as long as he was there to look after her. Polydectes resented this and told Perseus to prove his bravery by killing the dreadful gorgon, Medusa (*Meh-DOO-suh*).

Medusa

Medusa was one of three gorgon sisters. At one time Medusa had been a very beautiful girl, but she had boasted that she was more beautiful than the goddess Athena. Athena was very angry and changed Medusa's hair into snakes. Medusa's face remained as beautiful as always, but anyone who looked at her directly would be turned to stone. Perseus' task was therefore very difficult. However, the gods decided that they would help him. Hermes lent him his winged sandals to enable him to fly, Hades gave him a magic helmet, which made him invisible, and Artemis lent him her highly polished shield.

Only three people in the whole world knew where Medusa lived, and these were the Graeae (*GRAY-eye*), three horrible old women who had only one eye and one tooth, which they shared between them. Perseus intercepted the eye as the sisters passed it blindly to one another, and refused to return it until they told him where Medusa lived. Then he returned the eye and flew on to Medusa's lair in western Africa, where he found her asleep. Perseus knew that he must avoid looking at Medusa or he would be turned into stone. Using the polished shield as a mirror, he approached the sleeping Medusa without looking at her directly. Then he cut off her head with his sword, put it in a bag and flew off before her sisters could catch him.

Perseus and Andromeda

On his return journey, Perseus reached the northern coast of Africa, where he saw a maiden chained to a rock. Flying down to investigate, Perseus discovered that the girl was Andromeda

**An eighteenth-century painting depicting
Perseus and Andromeda by the German artist
Anton Raphael Mengs (1728–1779).**

(*An-DRAH-muh-duh*) who was to be
sacrificed to a sea monster preying on the
local people. The monster had been sent by
the gods because Andromeda's mother,
Cassiopeia (*Kass-EE-OH-pee-uh*), had boasted
that Andromeda was more beautiful than any
of the sea nymphs. After a dreadful struggle,
Perseus finally overcame the monster and
killed it. Andromeda's parents offered Perseus
any reward that he wanted. Perseus asked to
marry Andromeda and they joyfully agreed,
thinking that Andromeda could have no better
husband than the man who had saved her.
However, she had already been promised to
her uncle, Phineus (*Finn-EE-uss*), who tried to
take her by force. Perseus then pulled Medusa's head out of the bag he was carrying and
turned Phineus and his supporters into stone.

Theseus, the National Hero of Athens

Although Theseus (*THEE-see-uss*) was
mythical, the Athenians worshipped him as
the national hero of Athens and attributed
some important political reforms to him. In
particular, they claimed that Theseus created
the city-state of Athens.

It is true that at some point the various
communities in Attica were united into the
city-state of Athens, but we do not know
exactly when this happened, or who brought
it about. The Greeks liked to be able to
attribute specific events to specific people
(even mythical ones), which is why Theseus
was honored for uniting Athens.

The Death of Acrisius

Perseus now returned to the island of Seriphus and, when he discovered that King
Polydectes had been treating his mother poorly, turned Polydectes into stone, too. Perseus
then set off back to Argos, where he found that his grandfather, Acrisius, had been deposed
by a rival. Perseus restored Acrisius to his throne and forgave him for his treatment of
Danae. It seemed as if the family had been reunited happily, and that the prophecies of the
oracle would not come true.

However, one day Perseus and Acrisius were playing with a discus and a fierce wind blew
the discus toward Acrisius. The sharp edge struck his head and killed him at once. Perseus
was overcome with grief and left Argos for Mycenae, where he became the ruler of the city.

Theseus and the Minotaur

Theseus' father Aegeus (*Ee-GEE-uss*) was king of Athens and his mother was Princess Aethra
(*EE-thruh*) of Troezen (*TROYT-zeen*), in the Peloponnese (*Pell-oh-pon-NEES*). Aegeus was
forced to leave Aethra after the birth of Theseus but, before he went, he placed his sword
and sandals under a large boulder. He told Aethra that when Theseus was old enough and

strong enough to lift the boulder he must take Aegeus' sword and sandals and make his way to Athens. Aegeus promised that he would then acknowledge Theseus as his son and heir.

Adventures on the Road to Athens

Many years later, Theseus grew strong enough to lift the boulder and retrieve Aegeus' sword and sandals. He strapped them on and set out for Athens. Traveling was a dangerous business, as many robbers and thieves lay in wait to attack unwary travelers. Theseus dealt with several such robbers on his journey to Athens.

The first of these was the giant Periphetes (*Pear-ih-FEE-teez*) who was armed with a huge club and who attacked anyone who came into his path. Periphetes had killed many travelers in this way, but Theseus drove his sword deep into Periphetes' side and killed him. Theseus then took Periphetes' club and added it to his armory.

Shortly after this, Theseus came to Corinth where he heard about an extremely strong man called Sinis (*SIGH-niss*), who was nicknamed "The Pine-Bender." Sinis was called this because he enjoyed bending two tall pine trees down to the ground and then tying passersby to both the trees. He would then release the trees and, when they sprang upright, the traveler would be ripped apart. Theseus defeated Sinis in a fight and sent him to his death in exactly the same way.

Next, Theseus came to Megara, which was the home of the robber, Sciron (*SKY-ron*). He had his lair next to a

Left: This nineteenth-century bronze statuette shows Theseus battling the Minotaur.

Right: The neck of this wine jug, which dates to the seventh century B.C.E., shows the meeting of Ariadne and Theseus.

very narrow path on the cliffs and would force travelers to bend down to wash his feet. When they did so, Sciron would kick them off the path into the sea below, where there was a giant turtle that ate the bodies of Sciron's victims. Theseus forced Sciron to bend down to wash his feet, then kicked him off the path to drown and be devoured.

The last of Theseus' adventures on the way to Athens was to kill the cruel giant, Procrustes (*Pro-KRUS-teez*). Procrustes offered hospitality to any traveling strangers. However, when they wanted to go to bed, Procrustes would carry out his evil plan. He had one very short bed and one very long bed. He would force tall men to lie in the short bed and then cut off their limbs to make them fit the bed; short men were placed on the long bed and had their limbs stretched in a rack until they fitted. Theseus defeated Procrustes and treated him to the same torture.

This red-figure vase shows Theseus attacking the Minotaur. This vase was made in a Greek settlement in Sicily, Italy, between 470 and 460 B.C.E.

The Minotaur

When Theseus arrived at Athens, Aegeus was delighted to see his son. However, Athens was in mourning. Crete had defeated Athens in war, forcing Athens to provide seven young men and seven young women every year as a sacrifice to the Minotaur (*MINE-uh-tor*). The Minotaur was a fearsome monster with a bull's head and a man's body. It was the son of Pasiphae (*Pa-SIFF-aye*), the queen of Crete, and a bull. The gods had made her fall in love with the bull because Minos (*My-nuss*), the king of Crete, had not sacrificed to them properly. Minos was appalled by the monster and hid it away in an underground labyrinth built by the inventor Daedalus

(*DAID-uh-luss*). Theseus immediately offered to go with the victims to kill the monster. Aegeus did not want him to go, but Theseus said that it was his duty as a prince to free Athens from this dreadful annual sacrifice. Eventually, Aegeus agreed but, as Theseus embarked for Crete, Aegeus told him that the ship's sails were black because that was the color of mourning and grief. Theseus promised that if he survived he would change the black sails on his return to white ones so that all could see that he lived.

When Theseus reached Crete, the king's daughter, Ariadne (*Air-ee-AD-nee*), saw him and fell in love with him. She did not want him to die, so she smuggled in a sword, and some thread to help him find his way out of the labyrinth. Theseus tied the thread to the entrance and made his way into the maze, letting out the thread behind him. Soon he found and killed the Minotaur, and followed the thread back to the entrance. He and his companions then sailed away from Crete, taking Ariadne with them. However, by the time they had reached the island of Naxos (*NACK-suss*), Theseus had grown tired of Ariadne and abandoned her.

The god Dionysus fell in love with her and turned her into a constellation of stars, but the other gods were angry at Theseus' treatment of Ariadne. They caused Theseus to forget his promise to change the sails of the ship. Aegeus, who waited on the cliff every day for news of his son, saw the black sails on the horizon. Thinking that Theseus was dead, he threw himself into the sea. The Greeks believed that this was how the Aegean Sea got its name.

The Bones of Theseus

Later in life, Theseus became unpopular in Athens and eventually went into exile on the island of Scyros (*SKY-russ*) in the Aegean Sea, where he was murdered by King Lycomedes (*Lie-kuh-ME-deez*), who feared his strength. Although the story of Theseus was a myth, later Athenians were able to exploit the myth politically. They claimed that Athens had been united by a powerful man, so this justified Athens having a powerful empire.

An Athenian general dug up the bones of a very large man on the island of Scyros in the fifth century B.C.E. and brought them back to Athens, where they were honored as the bones of Theseus. Now the Athenians could not only boast about having a national hero, but also show off to other city-states that they possessed his remains.

This Roman mosaic shows Theseus fighting the Minotaur in the middle of the labyrinth.

Chapter Five

The Labors of Heracles

The Greeks believed in demi-gods, who were born of a god and a mortal. Heracles (*HAIR-uh-kleez*, known to the ancient Romans as Hercules) was one of the most popular of these demi-gods and many stories were told about him in Greek myth.

Heracles' Early Life

Heracles was the son of Zeus, the ruler of the gods, and Alcmene (*Alk-MAY-nee*), a mortal princess. Zeus' wife, Hera, was very angry that Zeus had fathered a child by another woman and vowed to kill the child. Summoning up two huge serpents with poisonous fangs, she sent them to the room where the infant Heracles lay in his cradle. However, the child saw the snakes, seized them by the neck and strangled them. Hera realized that she would not be able to destroy the baby, but decided to make his life as difficult as possible. She waited a long time for her revenge, but eventually saw the perfect opportunity. By this time, Heracles was happily married with children, but Hera drove him mad and, in a fit of insanity, he killed his wife and children. When Heracles recovered, he was overcome with grief and no longer wished to live in the world. However, the gods ordered that Heracles must be punished, and his punishment was to carry out twelve great labors, or tasks, for Eurystheus (*You-RISS-thee-uss*), the king of Mycenae and Argos (in the Peloponnese in southern Greece).

Heracles was set twelve great tasks as a punishment for killing his wife Megara and their children. One of Heracles' most challenging labors was to capture the three-headed dog Cerberus, which guarded the entrance to the Underworld.

The Nemean Lion was a fearsome creature and its hide was so tough that it could not be wounded by any weapon. Heracles strangled it and then used its skin as a cloak.

The Nemean Lion

Heracles' first task was to kill the Nemean (*NEE-me-un*) Lion, which was terrorizing the people of Nemea in the Peloponnese. Many people had tried to kill the lion before, but in vain. Its hide could not be penetrated by any weapon. Heracles was not afraid of the lion, so he entered its lair and strangled it. He then cut its skin open with its own claws and turned it into a fine cloak. When Eurystheus learned that Heracles had killed the lion, he was so terrified that he refused to allow Heracles to enter Mycenae for a long time.

The Hydra of Lerna

Heracles' second task was to kill the Hydra (*HIGH-druh*), which lived in a swamp at Lerna, near Argos. The Hydra was a monstrous snake with many heads. Whenever one head was cut off, many more grew in its place. Heracles asked his friend Iolaus (*Eye-oh-LAWS*) to help him by burning each stump as soon as he cut off a head. This meant that extra heads could not grow back on the stump. Finally, Heracles was able to sever the main head and the Hydra died. Heracles dipped his arrows in its blood. From then on Heracles' arrows inflicted lethal wounds, even if they had merely grazed the skin.

The Ceryneian Hind

The Hind of Ceryneia (*Ker-ee-NAY-uh*) was sacred to Artemis and had golden horns and bronze hooves. Heracles was ordered to capture it alive, but the animal could run so fast that it took Heracles a whole year to catch up with it. He then shot an arrow to pin together the hind's front legs, so that he did not kill it, but was able to pick it up and carry it back to Mycenae.

The Erymanthian Boar

The Erymanthian (*Air-uh-MAN-thee-un*) Boar was a huge, vicious animal, which lived in Arcadia, in the Peloponnese. Heracles forced it from a thicket where it was hiding. When it ran out, he chased it into a deep snowdrift and jumped on its back. He then bound it in chains and brought it back to King Eurystheus.

The Augean Stables

The king of Elis (*EE-liss*), named Augeas (*Aw-GEE-uss*), had a great number of cattle and oxen, which he kept in huge stables. The stables had never been cleaned and so were very dirty. Heracles was now ordered to clean them. It was impossible for one man, however strong, to clean them all, but Heracles used nature to help him in this task. He diverted the nearby river Alpheus (*AL-fee-uss*) from its course so that it ran through the stables and washed them clean. King Augeus claimed that it had been the river, not Heracles, which had completed the task, so Heracles killed him.

Heracles was a popular subject on Greek vase-paintings. This black-figure vase dates to the sixth century B.C.E.

The Stymphalian Birds

The Stymphalian (*Stim-FAY-lee-un*) Birds were a great flock of man-eating birds with bronze claws and beaks. They took their name from the Stymphalian Marsh where they lived. Heracles was unable to walk on the marsh and it was impossible to sail a boat through it. Since he could not attack them directly, he used trickery. Taking out a pair of bronze castanets, which Athena had given to him, he made so loud a noise that the birds flew up into the sky in fright. Heracles then shot as many birds as he could with his poison arrows, and the remainder flew away to the Isle of Ares in the Black Sea.

The Cretan Bull

Poseidon had given a huge bull to King Minos of Crete with orders that he was to sacrifice it to the gods. The animal was of amazing size and beauty, and Minos had not obeyed Poseidon, but had kept it within his own herds. Poseidon had therefore punished Minos by making the bull mad. It rampaged all over Crete causing great damage. It was very difficult for Heracles to overcome the bull, especially since it could breathe fire. However, Heracles eventually managed to capture it and bring it back to Eurystheus, who dedicated it to Hera.

Heracles could not attack the Cretan Bull from the front because it breathed fire. He seized it by its horns and overpowered it.

The Horses of Diomedes

King Diomedes (*Dye-oh-MEE-deez*) was a ruthless king of Thrace (*Thrayss*) who owned some very savage horses. Any stranger who came into his land was seized and fed to these horses. Heracles overpowered Diomedes' men and knocked Diomedes out with his club. He then fed Diomedes to his own horses. When they ate the flesh of their master they became tame, and Heracles led them back to Mycenae. The horses were then dedicated to Hera and set free.

This first-century C.E. mosaic from a Roman settlement in North Africa shows Heracles shooting the Stymphalian Birds with his poison arrows.

The Girdle of the Amazon Hippolyta

The Amazons were a fierce race. Unusually, the women were fearsome warriors, while the men carried out all of the household tasks. Their queen was Hippolyta (*Hih-POLL-i-tuh*) and she had a golden girdle, or belt, which had been given to her by Ares, the god of war. Eurystheus ordered Heracles to obtain this girdle for his daughter to wear.

Heracles traveled to the land of the Amazons and explained to Hippolyta why he had come. Hippolyta admired Heracles and promised to give him her girdle as a gift. However, Hera, who still hated Heracles, was angry that he was going to succeed in his task so easily and spread a rumor that Heracles had come to kidnap Hippolyta. The Amazons were very angry and attacked Heracles. He had to kill many of them before he was able to escape with the girdle.

The Cattle of Geryon

Geryon (*GAIR-ee-on*) was a hideous monster with three heads and three bodies joined together at the waist. He possessed some very fine cattle that were guarded by Orthrus (*ORR-thruss*), a

Every time that one head was cut from the Hydra, more grew back. This fifth-century B.C.E. **vase shows Heracles overcoming the Hydra with the help of his friend, Iolaus.**

two-headed watchdog, and Eurytion (*You-RIT-ee-on*), who was the son of Ares, the god of war. Heracles was now ordered to steal these cattle. Heracles killed Orthrus with his club and then slew Eurytion. Just as Heracles was beginning to drive off the cattle, Geryon appeared, raging in anger at Heracles' theft. Heracles cleverly shot a single arrow through all three of Geryon's bodies and killed him.

The Apple of the Hesperides

Heracles was now ordered to bring apples from the golden apple tree that had been given to Hera as a wedding present. Heracles had to make many journeys before he discovered that the tree was in the care of the Hesperides (*Hess-PAIR-i-deez*), who were the daughters of the evening and lived at the end of the world.

Heracles asked for help from Atlas, the giant who held up the heavens above the earth. Atlas was glad to help, but he told Heracles that he must take over his job while he was away. Heracles agreed and Atlas, released from his exhausting burden, went to the garden of the Hesperides. There he found a dragon called Ladon (*LAH-don*) curled around the tree, guarding the fruit. Atlas killed Ladon and plucked the fruit from the tree. When he came back to Heracles he refused to release him from holding up the sky. Heracles asked him to hold it for a moment while he placed a cushion on his back. Atlas agreed to do this, and was tricked into holding up the sky again. Heracles then traveled back to Eurystheus, who gave the apples to Athena.

The Capture of Cerberus

The most frightening of Heracles' Twelve Labors was to bring Cerberus (*SIR-buh-russ*), the three-headed hound, from the Underworld. Heracles first traveled across the river Styx (*Sticks*), which was the boundary between Earth and the Underworld. He then spoke to Hades about his task. Hades replied that he would let Heracles have Cerberus only if he defeated the hound with his bare hands. Heracles agreed, even though Cerberus' three heads were protected by manes of snakes and his tail was covered in sharp barbs. Heracles wrapped his impenetrable lion skin around himself and choked Cerberus until he gave in. Heracles then went back across the Styx and presented Cerberus to King Eurystheus. Eurystheus was so terrified by the sight of the hound that he leaped into a huge storage jar and refused to come out until Heracles had taken him back to the Underworld.

Cerberus was a terrifying hound who guarded the entry to the Underworld. He had three heads and a mane of snakes.

The death of Heracles. Heracles died in agony when he put on a shirt which had been treated with poison.

The Death of Heracles

Heracles was now free from all his labors, but his life did not end happily. During his adventures, Heracles had fallen in love with and married a woman called Deianeira (*Dye-uh-NEYE-ruh*). One day, when the two of them came to a swollen river, a centaur called Nessus (*NEH-suss*) offered to carry Deianeira across the torrent. Deianeira thanked Nessus and mounted his broad back. However, when Nessus reached the shore he did not stop to wait for Heracles to cross, but galloped off with Deianeira as his captive. Heracles heard his wife's screams and shot one of his deadly arrows at the centaur. As the centaur lay dying, he apologized to Deianeira and told her to take his shirt, which was stained with his blood. He told her that, if Heracles' love for her ever started to fade, she was to give the shirt to Heracles and he would immediately love her as much as ever.

Many years later, Heracles fell in love with a beautiful girl called Iole (*Eye-OH-lee*), and began neglecting his wife. Deianeira was very jealous, and decided that the time had come to use Nessus' shirt to win back her husband. However, Nessus had played a dreadful trick on her. When Heracles put on the shirt, he was not seized with love for his wife. Instead, a terrible burning pain ran through his body. He desperately tried to pull off the shirt, but it clung to his body, and he could not remove it. Heracles could not bear the pain, and resolved to die rather than live in agony. He built a huge funeral pyre, which he lit, and then flung himself into the flames. However, Zeus took pity on him. He came down from the heavens and bore Heracles off to Olympus to live there in happiness for all time.

Other Adventures of Heracles

Heracles was said to have had other adventures in between his Twelve Labors. One of these came as he returned from collecting the apples of the Hesperides. The gods Poseidon and Apollo had built the walls of Troy for King Laomedon (*Lay-AH-meh-don*), but he had refused to pay them what he had promised. In revenge the two gods sent a terrible monster to Troy, which ruined the fields and attacked the inhabitants.

Laomedon consulted an oracle, and was told that the gods would be appeased if he sacrificed his daughter, Hesione (*Heh-SIGH-o-nee*), to the monster. The Trojans forced Laomedon to carry out this command and, when Heracles came to Troy, he found Hesione bound to a rock, awaiting the arrival of the monster. Heracles offered to save Hesione if Laomedon would agree to give him two beautiful horses that Zeus had given him. Laomedon agreed, so Heracles killed the monster and saved Hesione. However, King Laomedon did not keep this promise either, so Heracles killed him and all his sons except little Priam, whose tears softened Heracles' heart. Priam was to grow up to be the king of Troy during the Trojan War.

Chapter Six

Love and Loss

Many of the Greek myths deal with classic difficulties faced by men and women across the centuries, such as love, death, and betrayal. The Greeks explained many of the problems faced by humankind as being due to the actions of the gods. They also used their gods to explain scientific matters, such as the changing seasons. While we no longer believe that Zeus or the other Greek gods control our actions, we can still enjoy the Greek myths for what they tell us about very important human emotions.

Persephone

Demeter was the goddess of crops and agriculture. She had one beautiful daughter called Persephone (*Per-SEH-foe-nee*) who loved to play with her friends on the slopes of Mount Etna in Sicily. One day Hades, the god of the Underworld, saw her playing and fell in love with her. He felt that if only Persephone would come and live with him, his life in the land of the dead would be much happier. When he approached Persephone, she screamed and tried to flee. However, Hades snatched her up and carried her down to the Underworld in his chariot.

When Demeter returned from the fields she searched far and wide for her daughter, but there was no trace of the girl. When Demeter was told that Persephone had been snatched by Hades, she was heartbroken and no longer cared for the earth and the crops. Soon the earth stopped producing fruit and corn, and the people were faced with famine. In despair, they begged Zeus to restore Persephone to her mother so that Demeter would look after the crops again. Zeus promised to do this if Persephone had

Orpheus was devastated when he discovered that his beloved wife Eurydice had died from a snakebite. He set off to the Underworld to try to bring her back to life.

Greek Views on the Environment

The Greeks used the myth of Persephone to explain the changing agricultural seasons. When Persephone was in the land of the living, Demeter was happy and the crops grew, but when Persephone returned to Hades, Demeter grieved and autumn and winter came to the earth.

The Greeks also thought that it was very important to keep the gods happy by building them temples and offering them sacrifices. In a largely agricultural society, Demeter was a very important goddess. This explains why there are so many Greek temples dedicated to Demeter or Persephone. Similarly, the god of the sea, Poseidon, attracted much attention from seafarers. They feared that, if they did not sacrifice to Poseidon, their ships would sink in rough seas or storms.

This clay relief dates from around 460 B.C.E. and comes from the sanctuary of Aphrodite and Persephone in the Greek city-state of Locri (southern Italy). It shows Persephone and Hades, holding crops. Agriculture was a very important part of Greek life and goddesses associated with crops were very popular with Greek farmers.

not eaten any food while she was in the Underworld. Persephone had eaten six pomegranate seeds while she was with Hades, so Zeus decided that she must live in the Underworld for six months of the year.

Orpheus and Eurydice

Orpheus (*OAR-fee-us*) was the son of Apollo and the muse Calliope (*Kuh-LIE-oh-pee*). Orpheus inherited his father's musical talent and his mother's poetic ability, and soon became the most famous of all musicians. He married a beautiful woman called Eurydice (*You-RID-iss-ee*), and they loved each other passionately. Tragically, Eurydice died after being bitten by a snake, and Orpheus was heartbroken. He begged Zeus to allow him to go to the Underworld to look for his wife. Zeus said that he could, but warned him of the dangers he would face.

When Orpheus arrived, he met Cerberus, the three-headed hound which guarded the entrance to the Underworld. Orpheus lifted up his lyre and played such beautiful music that Cerberus was lulled to sleep. Orpheus then entered and explained his mission to the god of the Underworld, Hades. Hades was moved by Orpheus' love for Eurydice. He permitted Orpheus to lead her back to the upper world. However, Orpheus was told that he must on no account look back to see if his wife was following him. If he did so, she would be returned immediately to the Underworld forever. Orpheus had nearly reached the Earth when he turned around to see whether Eurydice was there. She was, but that was Orpheus' last sight of her. He had broken his agreement with Hades, and so she had to return to the ghosts of the Underworld for eternity. Orpheus spent the rest of his life sadly wandering, searching for his wife. Eventually,

Orpheus went to the Underworld to bring back his wife, Eurydice. This painting by Jan Brueghel the Elder (1568–1625) shows Orpheus turning around just before Eurydice has reached Earth.

The Muses

The Greeks believed that there were nine muses (female goddesses) who looked after different areas of literature, music, and intellectual achievement. The Greeks believed that the muses were daughters of Zeus and Mnemosyne (*NE-moh-sin-ee*). The Greek word "museum" originally meant "a place of the muses" and has come to mean a place where knowledge is housed.

Calliope (*Kuh-LIE-oh-pee*—epic poetry)
Clio (*KLEE-oh*—history)
Erato (*E-RAH-toe*—lyric poetry)
Euterpe (*You-TER-pee*—love poetry)
Melpomene (*Mel-POM-in-ee*—tragedy)
Polyhymnia (*POLLY-him-nee-uh*—hymns)
Terpsichore (*Turp-SI-kuh-ree*—dancing)
Thalia (*Tha-LAY-uh*—comedy)
Urania (*You-RAY-nee-uh*—astronomy)

The nine muses dancing with the god Apollo, who can be recognized by his bow and arrows.

some women ordered him to play joyful music, which he could no longer do. They became so enraged that they tore him apart. Even in death, as his head floated down a river, he called out for his lost love, Eurydice.

Hero and Leander

Hero was a beautiful priestess of Aphrodite in the town of Sestos (*SESS-toss*). Sestos was built on a narrow strip of land called the Chersonese (*KER-suh-neez*), which is divided by the waters of the Hellespont (*HELL-us-pont*) from Ionia (the northwest section of modern Turkey). Rumors of Hero's beauty spread throughout the region. Eventually, a young man called Leander (*Lee-AN-der*) came from his hometown of Abydos (*Uh-BY-dawss*) to catch sight of the beautiful priestess. When he entered the temple he was captivated by Hero's beauty and immediately fell deeply in love with her. Hero was also struck by the young man's appearance and soon was equally in love with him. However, she knew that her parents would never agree to their marriage, and begged him to leave her. Leander refused to do so until he had learned where she lived. He then promised that he would swim across the Hellespont by night and visit Hero without anyone learning that he had come. Hero promised to leave a lamp burning to signal the direction in which he should swim.

Each night, Leander swam across the Hellespont to be with his beloved. Each morning, he swam back to the other shore. One day, there was a fierce storm, and Hero begged Leander to stay with her all day. However, Leander did not want anyone to discover him and said that he would return to Abydos and swim back by night. When evening came, the storm had become more violent. Hero had tried to persuade Leander not to attempt the night swim if the sea was too rough, but Leander could not face spending a night away from her. He set out from the shore as usual, but soon began to weaken. He looked up to search for Hero's guiding light, but the storm had blown it out. Exhausted and not knowing where to go, Leander sank beneath the waves and drowned. After a sleepless night of worry, Hero found his body floating on the water. Distraught with grief, she flung herself into the Hellespont and drowned alongside her lover.

Eros and Psyche

Psyche (*SIGH-key*) was the youngest and most beautiful of three sisters. Many people believed that she was more beautiful than Aphrodite. Psyche denied that she could be more beautiful than a goddess, but Aphrodite was determined to punish her. Aphrodite therefore sent her son, Eros (*AIR-ohs*, known to the Romans as Cupid, the god of love), to kill her with an arrow. However, Eros was taken aback by her beauty

A detail from the famous statue of Cupid and Psyche by Antonio Canova (1757–1822) in the Louvre, Paris.

and cut himself on his own arrow. The potion on the arrow caused him to fall deeply in love with Psyche.

Eros asked the South Wind to carry Psyche away to a distant island. When she woke up, she found herself in a beautiful garden. Hidden voices reassured her that she was safe and asked her to enter a palace in the grounds of the garden. There hidden servants looked after her until dusk. When night came, Eros approached Psyche and told her of his love for her. Psyche could not see him, but listened to his kind voice and soon fell in love with him. Eros told her that she must not try to look at his face or find out his name because, if she did so, he would have to leave her forever.

For a long time, Eros and Psyche were very happy together. Psyche could not wait for the days to pass, since Eros could visit her only at night. But one day Psyche met her elder sisters, who were envious of her happiness. They told Psyche that her lover must be a horrible monster if he could not show her his face. Psyche became very worried and decided that she must find out who Eros was. That night, she lit an oil lamp, crept into the bedroom, and held the lamp above Eros. When she saw him for the first time, she was so overwhelmed with love and pride that she forgot to be careful. A drop of oil spilled from the lamp and fell onto Eros' shoulder. With a cry he leaped up from the bed and fled from Psyche.

Psyche was wretchedly unhappy at the loss of Eros and tried to kill herself, but the gods would not allow this. Instead they compelled her to work as one of Aphrodite's servants. Eventually, after many years, Zeus took pity on the lovers and reunited them.

Daedalus and Icarus

Daedalus was the famous inventor who was said to have built the labyrinth in which the Minotaur lived (*see* Chapter Four). However, although Daedalus had worked hard for King Minos of Crete, the king refused to let him and his son Icarus (*IK-uh-russ*) leave the island. Daedalus did not have a ship and no Cretan was allowed to lend him one. Therefore,

The Influence of Greek Myth on Western Civilization

The myths in this volume were not true stories, but were told by the ancient Greeks partly to explain natural events (such as the seasons) and partly to show that human matters rarely went according to plan. These amazing tales provided the inspiration for some of the greatest Greek writers. In turn, the writings of these Greek authors have had a huge influence on modern society. Many things, from brand names (such as Nike, which means "victory") to great works of art, have their origin in the stories of ancient Greece. The finest writers, artists, composers, and thinkers of the world (such as Shakespeare, Racine, Goethe, Michelangelo, Leonardo da Vinci, Mozart, and Schubert) have all drawn inspiration from ancient Greece and the Greeks.

Icarus fell to the sea when he flew too close to the sun and the wax that held the feathers on his wings melted. In this seventeenth-century painting, Daedalus watches in horror as his son plummets to his death.

Daedalus had to invent another method of escape. He collected a great many birds' feathers and fixed them onto frames with wax. Then he attached the frames to his and his son's shoulders and they prepared to fly away. Before they did so, he warned Icarus that he must on no account fly too high because the heat of the sun would melt the wax. Icarus promised that he would take care but, after he had been flying for some time, he was so delighted with his new skill that he forgot his father's warnings and soared up toward the sun. The heat of the rays melted the wax and the feathers fell apart. Icarus plunged down into the sea and drowned.

The Story of Alcestis

Alcestis (*Al-KESS-tiss*) was the wife of King Admetus (*Ad-ME-tuss*). Admetus was a powerful king, but he feared dying. However, he had been promised by the god Apollo that, when the time came for him to die, he would be spared if a member of his family was prepared to die in his place. When the hour of his death approached, Admetus begged his aged parents to die in his place. They refused. Then he asked other relatives and they also refused. However, Alcestis loved her husband passionately and wished to save him. Therefore she willingly took poison in order that he should live. Admetus was extremely unhappy when he realized that his beloved wife was dying. Fortunately, the hero Heracles, who was a friend of Admetus, happened to be visiting him. When Heracles discovered what Alcestis had done, he made his way to the Underworld and rescued her. Admetus and Alcestis were then reunited and as a reward for their love for each other the gods spared both of their lives.

Glossary of Names

Absyrtus younger brother of Medea

Achilles Greek hero in the Trojan War

Acrisius king of Argos, father of Danae

Aeetes king of Colchis, owner of the Golden Fleece

Aegeus king of Athens, father of Theseus

Aegisthus cousin of Agamemnon, beloved by Clytemnestra

Aeneas one of the few Trojans who escaped the sacking of Troy, believed by the ancient Romans to be their ancestor

Aeolus king of the winds

Aeson father of Jason, brother of Pelias

Aethra mother of Theseus

Agamemnon older brother of Menelaus

Alcinous king of the Phaeacians, father of Nausicaa

Alcmene mother of Heracles

Andromache wife of Hector

Andromeda daughter of Cassiopeia, rescued by Perseus from sacrifice to a sea monster

Aphrodite goddess of love

Apollo god of the sun, in earlier times also called Helios

Ares god of war

Ariadne daughter of Minos and Pasiphae

Artemis goddess of hunting and the moon, sister of Apollo

Astyanax son of Hector and Andromache

Athena goddess of war, arts and crafts, and wisdom

Atlas god condemned to hold up the heavens as punishment for rebelling against Zeus

Augeas king of Elis whose stables Heracles cleaned by diverting a river

Briseis slave of Achilles, taken by Agamemnon

Calchas prophet of the Greek army during the Trojan War

Calliope muse of poetry

Calypso nymph with whom Odysseus stayed for many years

Cassandra daughter of Priam, enslaved by Agamemnon

Cassiopeia mother of Andromeda

Cerberus the three-headed hound of Hades

Chiron centaur who brought up the young Jason

Chryseis daughter of Chryses, enslaved by Agamemnon

Chryses priest of Apollo, father of Chryseis

Circe enchantress who temporarily turned some of Odysseus' men into pigs

Clytemnestra wife of Agamemnon, mother of Orestes and Electra

Croesus king of Lydia, defeated by the Persians

Daedalus inventor from Crete, father of Icarus

Danae daughter of Acrisius, mother of Perseus

Deianeira wife of Heracles

Demeter goddess of crops and fertility, mother of Persephone

Diomedes king of Thrace, defeated by Heracles

Dionysus god responsible for wine and drama, son of Zeus and Semele

Electra daughter of Agamemnon and Clytemnestra, sister of Orestes

Eris goddess of discord

Eros god of love, son of Aphrodite

Erymanthian Boar an enormous boar captured by Heracles for King Eurystheus

Eumaeus Odysseus' swineherd

Euripides playwright

Eurydice wife of Orpheus

Eurylochus one of Odysseus' men who resisted Circe

Eurystheus king of Mycenae and Argos

Eurytion son of Ares

Gaia the earth, one of the two creation gods

Geryon a monster with three heads and three bodies

Hades god of the Underworld

Hector son of Priam and Hecuba

Hecuba wife of Priam, mother of Hector

Helen wife of Menelaus

Helios god of the sun

Hephaestus god of fire, blacksmith to the gods

Hera goddess of childbirth, women, and marriage, wife of Zeus

Heracles demi-god, son of Zeus and Alcmene

Hermes messenger of the gods, son of Zeus and Maia

Hero priestess of Aphrodite, beloved of Leander

Hesione daughter of Laomedon, saved from sacrifice by Heracles

Hesperides daughters of the evening

Hestia goddess of the hearth

Hippolyta queen of the Amazons, a warrior tribe of women

Hydra giant, many-headed snake, defeated by Heracles

Icarus son of Daedalus, drowned after flying too close to the sun

Iolaus friend of Heracles, who helped him overcome the Hydra

Iole girl with whom Heracles falls in love

Iphigenia daughter of Agamemnon, sacrificed to the gods for a fair wind

Jason leader of the Argonauts

Kronos, leader of the Titans, son of Gaia and Uranus, father of Zeus

Ladon dragon who guarded the golden apple tree of the Hesperides

Laocoon Trojan priest of Poseidon

Laomedon king of Troy who broke his promises, defeated by Heracles

Leander beloved of Hero

Leto mother of Apollo and Artemis

Lycomedes king of Scyros

Maia daughter of Atlas

Medea daughter of Aeetes, brother of Absyrtus, said to be a witch

Medusa a beautiful gorgon, would turn to stone anyone who looked directly at her face

Menelaus king of Sparta, brother of Agamemnon, husband of Helen

Minos king of Crete, married to Pasiphae

Minotaur a monster with a bull's head and a man's body

Myrtilus son of Hermes

Nausicaa daughter of Alcinous, helped Odysseus

Nemean Lion a lion with an impenetrable hide, which Heracles turned into a cloak

Nessus a centaur who tricked Deianeira into killing Heracles

Odysseus king of Ithaca, fought in the Trojan War and planned the trick of the Trojan Horse

Orestes son of Agamemnon, brother of Electra

Orpheus musician, son of Apollo and Calliope

Orthrus two-headed watchdog

Paris prince of Troy, abducted Helen

Pasiphae wife of Minos, mother of the Minotaur

Patroclus friend of Achilles

Peleus husband of Thetis

Pelias brother of Aeson, seized his kingdom from him

Pelops son of Tantalus, restored to life after his father killed him

Penelope wife of Odysseus, mother of Telemachus

Periphetes giant, killed by Theseus

Persephone daughter of Demeter, beloved of Hades

Perseus son of Danae and Zeus, killed Medusa

Phineus Andromeda's uncle, to whom she was promised in marriage

Polydectes king of the island of Seriphus, fell in love with Danae

Polyphemus cyclops, defeated by Odysseus

Poseidon god of the sea, earthquakes, and horses, brother of Zeus and Hades

Priam king of Troy, husband of Hecuba, father of Hector

Procrustes giant, defeated by Theseus

Psyche beloved of Eros

Rhea sister and husband of Kronos, mother of Zeus

Sciron robber, defeated by Theseus

Scylla man-eating monster with six heads and twelve feet

Semele mother of Dionysus

Sinis strong man, defeated by Theseus

Sinon Greek soldier left behind to inform the Trojans about the Trojan Horse

Stymphalian Birds man-eating birds with bronze claws and beaks

Tantalus father of Pelops

Telemachus son of Odysseus and Penelope

Theseus hero and king of Athens

Thetis sea nymph, wife of Peleus

Tiresias seer, or prophet

Uranus the sky, one of the two creation gods

Zeus ruler of the gods, responsible for law, justice, and the protection of families, brother of Hades and Poseidon

Glossary

Acheron the river of woe, one of five rivers said to separate the Underworld from the world of the living

acropolis the fortified part of a city, built on high ground

altar a raised surface on which rituals or sacrifices are carried out

ambassador a person who represents his nation or state, often traveling abroad

argonauts those who sailed with Jason on the ship *Argo*

Charybdis whirlpool close to where the monster Scylla lived

cyclops a one-eyed giant

deity a god

demi-god the child of a god and a mortal

entrails the inner parts of an animal

festival a special day when there may be feasting and other celebrations or entertainment

fury a vengeful spirit

gorgon a female monster with snakes for hair

graeae sisters of the gorgons; three old women who shared a single eye between them

immortal someone who lives forever, such as a god

labyrinth a maze; the Minotaur was kept in a labyrinth on Crete

libation a liquid poured onto the ground or into a bowl or cup as an offering

lyre a stringed musical instrument

moly a black flower Odysseus used as protection from Circe's magic powers

mortal a being, for example a human, whose life will eventually come to an end

muse one of nine goddesses linked with human creativity and achievement

nymph a minor goddess, closely connected with nature, such as water or trees

oracle a shrine where the future may be foretold

pyre a fire to burn the bodies of the dead

Pythia a priestess of Apollo, who hears the oracle speak

seafarers people who travel on the sea, usually for trade or war

seer a prophet; one who can foretell events

siren a creature with the face of a girl but the body of a bird; sings to draw men to their death by drowning

Styx the river of hate, one of five rivers said to separate the Underworld from the world of the living

tablet a flat surface on which people write

temple a building used for prayer and worship

thyrsus a magic stick topped with a pine cone and covered in ivy and vines, carried by Dionysus and his followers

trident a three-pronged spear, such as that carried by Poseidon

Underworld the land of the dead, ruled by Hades

Learn More About

Books

Ancient Greece (DK Eyewitness Books). New York: Dorling Kindersley, 2004.

Ashworth, Leon. Gods and Goddesses of Ancient Greece. London: Cherrytree Books, 2005.

Khanduri, Kamini. Tales of the Trojan War. New York: Scholastic, 2005.

Lines, Kathleen (ed.). The Faber Book of Greek Legends. Boston: Faber, 2001.

Lister, Robin. The Odyssey. Boston: Kingfisher, 2003.

Macdonald, Fiona. Gods and Goddesses in the Daily Life of the Ancient Greeks. Columbus, Ohio: P. Bendrick, 2002.

McCarty, Nick. The Iliad. Boston: Kingfisher, 2004.

Powell, Anton. Ancient Greece (Cultural Atlas for Young People). Philadelphia, Pennsylvania: Chelsea House Publications, 2007.

Sutcliff, Rosemary. Black Ships Before Troy. New York: Laurel Leaf, 2005.

Web Sites

About.com—Olympian Gods and Goddesses
http://ancienthistory.about.com/cs/mytholympians/

Encyclopedia Mythica
www.pantheon.org/areas/mythology/europe/greek

Greece Museums
www.ancient-greece.org/museum.html

HistoryWiz—Ancient Greece
www.historywiz.com/anc-greece.htm

TeacherOz—Greeks
www.teacheroz.com/greeks.html

ThinkQuest—Greek Mythology
http://library.thinkquest.org/J0110010/home.htm

University of Pennsylvania—The Ancient Greek World
http://www.museum.upenn.edu/Greek_World/index.html

Mythweb—Greek Mythology
www.mythweb.com

Quoted Sources

p. 25—Euripides, Iphigenia in Aulis, lines 1368–1473

p. 27—Homer, Iliad, Book 22, lines 312–363 (abridged)

p. 40—Homer, Odyssey, Book 11, lines 150–208 (abridged)

Index

Page numbers in italics refer to images and captions